EMBODIED HEALING:

A COMPREHENSIVE GUIDE TO SOMATIC THERAPY

Effective Techniques for Integrating Mind, Body, and Spirit in Therapy for Anxiety Relief and Stress Reduction.

Dr.Lizzy Darlington

Table of contents

INTRODUCTION   **5**

Chapter 1: Understanding somatic therapy   **11**

Techniques in Somatic Therapy   13

Origins and Principles of Somatic Therapy.   17

The Mental-Body-Spirit Connection   22

Advantages of Somatic Therapy for Anxiety and Stress Relief   25

Chapter 2: The Effects of Trauma and Stress **30**

Examining Trauma and Stress Responses   34

The impact of trauma on the body and nervous system   37

Understanding Chronic Stress and Its Effects 40

Chapter 3: Foundations of Somatic Healing   **44**

Body Awareness and Sensations   47

Techniques for breathing and anchoring   49

Expressive Gratitude in Somatic Orientation   55

Chapter 4:Interventions using Somatics to Reduce Anxiety   **60**

Progressive Muscular Relaxation (PMR):   66

Breathwork Techniques for Nervous System Regulation   69

Progressive Muscle Relaxation Techniques.   74

Chapter 5: Exploring Mind-Body Connections 79

Mindfulness Meditation for Stress Reduction. 83

Body Scanning and Sensory Awareness Activities   88

Emotion Regulation Strategies Through

Somatic Awareness   93

Chapter 6: Combining Neuroscience and Psychology   99

Combining Neuroscience and Integration: 101

Recognizing the Link Between the Brain and Body   104

Integrating Somatic Approaches with Cognitive Behavioral Therapy   113

Chapter 7: Case Studies: Healing with Somatic Therapy   119

True Stories of Transformation and Growth. 124

Example of Somatic Techniques in Practice 129

.Readers' Perspectives on "Embodied Healing"   132

Chapter 8: Cultural Sensitivity and Inclusiveness in Somatic Therapy   138

Honouring the Diversity of Trauma and Healing   143

Adapting Somatic Practices to Various Cultural Contexts   148

Ethical Considerations for Cross-Cultural Somatic Work   152

Chapter 9: Self-Care Practices for Somatic Awareness.   158

Developing Resilience and Self-Compassion.   162

Rituals of Grounding and Centering   166

Strategies to Maintain Boundaries and Prevent Burnout   170

Conclusion: Embracing Embodied Healing: Empowering You to Embody Wellness and Thrive   175

INTRODUCTION

Somatic therapy traces its roots to various disciplines and philosophies that recognize the inseparable connection between the mind, body, and spirit. While the term "somatic therapy" gained popularity in the 20th century, its principles have ancient origins, dating back to ancient healing practices in cultures around the world. From indigenous healing rituals to Eastern traditions like yoga and tai chi, the idea of embodied healing has been a fundamental aspect of human wellness for centuries.

The modern development of somatic therapy can be attributed to pioneers such as Wilhelm Reich, Moshe Feldenkrais, and Alexander Lowen, who explored the interplay between bodily sensations, emotional experiences, and psychological well-being. Their work laid the groundwork for contemporary approaches to somatic therapy, which integrate insights from psychology, neuroscience, and holistic health modalities.

Central to somatic therapy is the recognition of the intricate relationship between the mind and body. Unlike traditional talk therapies that focus primarily on verbal communication, somatic therapy acknowledges that emotional experiences are stored not only in the mind but also in the body. Traumatic events, chronic stress, and unresolved emotions can manifest as physical symptoms, tension patterns, and somatic sensations.

By attending to bodily sensations, movement patterns, and nonverbal cues, somatic therapists aim to access and address the root causes of psychological distress. Through gentle exploration, guided awareness, and somatic interventions, individuals can uncover and release stored tension, repressed emotions, and traumatic memories held within the body.

The primary goal of somatic therapy is to facilitate holistic healing and integration by restoring harmony between the mind, body, and spirit. By cultivating somatic awareness and facilitating the release of tension and trauma, somatic therapy offers a pathway to greater resilience, self-regulation, and emotional well-being.

One of the key benefits of somatic therapy is its effectiveness in alleviating symptoms of anxiety, stress, and trauma-related disorders. Research has shown that somatic interventions such as breathwork, movement therapy, and body-centred awareness practices can help regulate the autonomic nervous system, reduce physiological arousal, and promote relaxation responses.

Furthermore, somatic therapy fosters a deeper sense of self-awareness, embodied presence, and attunement to one's inner wisdom. By reconnecting with the sensations, emotions, and felt experiences of the body, individuals can cultivate greater self-compassion, acceptance, and empowerment in their healing journey.

In today's fast-paced and digitally driven world, the need for embodied healing has never been greater. The prevalence of chronic stress, trauma, and mental health challenges underscores the importance of holistic approaches that address the root causes of suffering and promote sustainable well-being.

"Embodied Healing: A Comprehensive Guide to Somatic Therapy" seeks to fill a crucial gap in the literature by offering readers a practical roadmap for integrating somatic principles into their lives. Whether you are a therapist, healthcare professional, or individual seeking personal growth, this book provides valuable insights, techniques, and resources for harnessing the transformative power of somatic therapy.

In the pages that follow, we will explore a wide range of somatic techniques, exercises, and practices designed to promote relaxation, resilience, and self-discovery. Through case studies, reflections, and practical exercises, readers will learn how to cultivate greater somatic awareness, regulate their nervous systems, and embark on a journey of embodied healing and transformation.

Chapter 1: Understanding somatic therapy

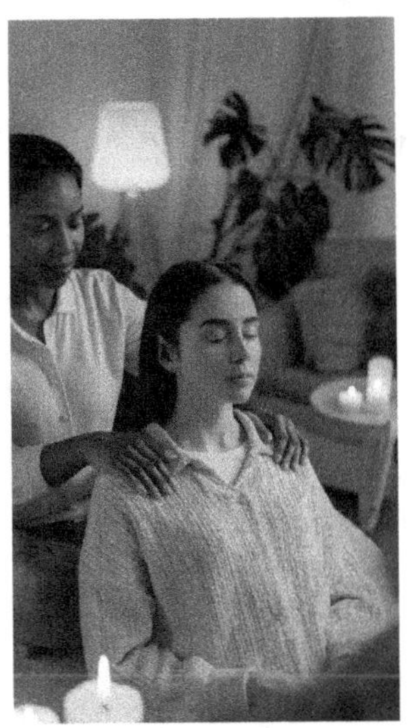

Somatic therapy is a comprehensive approach to healing that respects the interconnectedness of the mind, body, and spirit. In this part, we'll look at the fundamental ideas, procedures, and aims of somatic therapy, giving you a better grasp of its transformational power.

The Somatic Therapy Principles

At the basis of somatic therapy is the underlying belief that our bodies contain significant knowledge and information about our emotional experiences and psychological well-being. Unlike conventional talk treatments, which rely heavily on verbal communication, somatic therapy recognizes that emotions are perceived not just in the mind but also in the body. Somatic therapists assist people in accessing and processing deeply held emotions and traumas hidden inside their bodies by focusing on physical sensations, movement patterns, and nonverbal signs.

Techniques in Somatic Therapy

Somatic therapy uses a wide range of approaches and treatments to facilitate healing and integration on a physical, emotional, and spiritual level. These strategies could include:

1. Breathwork: Breathwork exercises are an important part of somatic therapy because they help people regulate their nervous systems, decrease tension, and achieve states of calm and present. Deep belly breathing, coherent breathing, and breath awareness are all effective techniques for improving emotional well-being and inner balance.

2. Body Awareness: Developing somatic awareness entails being observant of physical feelings, movements, and postures. Individuals learn to tune into their bodies' subtle signals and messages via activities like body scanning, gradual relaxation, and mindful movement, resulting in increased self-awareness and self-regulation.

3. Movement Therapy: Yoga, dance therapy, and tai chi are all essential components of somatic therapy. These techniques enable people to explore their bodies via movement, enabling the release, expression, and integration of emotions hidden inside them. Movement therapy is especially beneficial in trauma recovery because it provides a nonverbal technique of processing and releasing emotional energy.

4. Somatic experience: Peter Levine developed somatic experience, a body-oriented approach to trauma rehabilitation. Individuals may restructure painful memories and release energy held in their nervous systems by gently exploring physical sensations and activation patterns. Somatic experiences seek to reestablish a feeling of safety, empowerment, and resilience in the face of trauma.

Somatic Therapy Goals

Somatic therapy's main purpose is to promote comprehensive healing and integration by restoring balance to the mind, body, and spirit. Individuals may experience remarkable changes in their physical, emotional, and spiritual well-being by developing somatic awareness, regulating the nervous system, and releasing accumulated stress and trauma.

Individuals may attain the following aims with somatic therapy:

- **Relief from Physical problems:** Somatic treatment may help with a variety of physical problems, including chronic pain, muscular tension, and psychosomatic diseases. Individuals may get long-term relief and physical health restoration by addressing the underlying emotional and psychological causes that contribute to these symptoms.

- **Emotional Regulation**: Somatic therapy provides people with skills and strategies to better manage their emotions. Individuals who learn to recognize, express, and manage their emotions may have increased emotional resilience, stability, and energy in their life.

- **Healing Trauma:** Somatic therapy provides a gentle and compassionate approach to trauma recovery. Individuals may break free from the hold of prior traumas by carefully exploring and processing painful memories and feelings, regaining a sense of safety, empowerment, and completeness.

Origins and Principles of Somatic Therapy.

Somatic therapy is founded on a combination of traditional healing traditions and current psychological findings, stressing the interdependence of the mind and body in the process of healing and self-discovery. Let's look at the history and beliefs that support this transformational approach to wellbeing.

Ancient Wisdom and Modern Psychology

Somatic therapy dates back to ancient societies that acknowledged the body's tremendous effect on emotional well-being and spiritual progress. Yoga, meditation, and traditional bodywork techniques like massage and acupuncture have long recognized the complex relationship between physical sensations, emotional emotions, and general health.

In the twentieth century, pioneers in psychology and holistic medicine started to delve further into the mind-body relationship. Wilhelm Reich, Moshe Feldenkrais, and Alexander Lowen pioneered systems that combined psychological ideas with somatic awareness and movement-based treatments. Their work paved the way for what would eventually be recognized as somatic therapy.

The Somatic Therapy Principles

Somatic therapy, unlike typical talk treatments, is based on three essential principles:

1. Embodied Presence: Somatic treatment stresses the significance of being completely present in the body, including being aware of physical sensations, movements, and postures. Individuals may get vital insights about their emotions, needs, and inner experiences by tuning into their body's felt sense.

2. Holistic Integration: Somatic treatment sees the person as a whole, acknowledging the interdependence of physical, emotional, mental, and spiritual components. Rather than treating symptoms in isolation, somatic therapy tries to address the root causes of imbalance and discord at all levels of being.

3. Nonverbal Communication: Unlike conventional talk treatments, which concentrate mostly on verbal discourse, somatic therapy recognizes the importance of nonverbal communication in the therapeutic process. Emotions, memories, and relationship dynamics are communicated not just verbally, but also via body movements, face expressions, and somatic sensations.

4. Trauma-Informed Approach: Somatic therapy takes a trauma-informed approach to recovery, acknowledging the widespread effect of trauma on the body and nervous system. Individuals are helped to safely process and integrate traumatic experiences held in their bodies via gentle investigation and somatic therapies.

5. Empowerment and Self-Agency: Somatic therapy promotes a feeling of empowerment and self-determination throughout the healing process. Somatic therapy helps people recover their health, vitality, and well-being by helping them to build self-awareness, self-regulation, and self-compassion.

Somatic therapists establish a safe and supportive environment for people to go on a path of self-discovery, healing, and change by acknowledging and incorporating these concepts into their therapeutic practice. Individuals may discover deeper levels of themselves, release patterns of stress and trauma, and reconnect with their intrinsic ability for wholeness and resilience by practising somatic awareness, movement-based therapies, and embodied presence.

- **Enhanced Self-Awareness:** Somatic therapy helps people get a better awareness of themselves and their inner worlds. Individuals achieve clarity, insight, and self-compassion by being more aware of their physiological sensations, emotions, and inner knowledge.

Overall, somatic therapy provides a deep route of healing and change, helping people to regain their health, vitality, and completeness on all levels of their being.

The Mental-Body-Spirit Connection

The mind-body-spirit link is crucial to holistic therapeutic approaches, such as somatic therapy. It acknowledges that humans are complex systems with interwoven physical, mental, emotional, and spiritual qualities. In this part, we'll look at how these dimensions interact and impact one other, influencing our experiences, health, and well-being.

The physical dimension is the most palpable aspect of our bodies, including its structures, functions, feelings, and motions. Diet, exercise, sleep, and the environment all have an impact on our physical health. Somatic therapy focuses on body sensations, symptoms, and tension patterns because they typically reflect underlying emotional and psychological states.

The mental dimension includes our ideas, beliefs, perceptions, and cognitive processes. Stress, trauma, coping techniques, and our worldview all have an impact on our mental health. Mental patterns and narratives are investigated in somatic therapy using verbal conversation, introspection, and cognitive restructuring approaches, since they may have an influence on our physical and emotional health.

The emotional component refers to our feelings, emotions, and affective states. Relationships, life experiences, coping strategies, and self-awareness all have an impact on our emotional well-being. Emotions are recognized as embodied experiences in somatic therapy, with body sensations, movements, and facial expressions used to communicate them. Individuals who access and resolve emotions stored in their bodies might enjoy better emotional resilience and well-being.

The spiritual dimension includes our feeling of purpose, connection, and transcendence. It includes beliefs, values, existential concerns, and feelings of awe and wonder. Somatic therapy recognizes the spiritual dimension as an important component of human experience, leading people toward better connection with their true selves and higher truths.

Integration in Somatic Therapy: Somatic therapy acknowledges the interdependent role of the mind, body, and spirit in forming our experiences and fostering healing. Somatic therapy provides a comprehensive approach to well-being by treating all aspects of the human being—physical, mental, emotional, and spiritual. This develops integration, completeness, and vitality on all levels of our being. Individuals may create increased self-awareness, resilience, and alignment with their actual selves via mind-body-spirit activities, eventually leading to significant change and progress.

Advantages of Somatic Therapy for Anxiety and Stress Relief

Somatic therapy takes a comprehensive approach to anxiety and stress relief by treating the underlying causes and developing increased self-awareness, relaxation, and resilience. Let's look at some of the important advantages that somatic therapy offers for anxiety and stress relief:

1. Embodied Awareness: Somatic treatment teaches people to become acutely aware of their physical feelings, movements, and postures. Individuals become more aware of the bodily signs of worry and stress when they focus on the present moment and cultivate body awareness. This increased awareness enables them to act early and use somatic approaches to reduce symptoms before they worsen.

2. Nervous System Regulation: One of the fundamental aims of somatic therapy is to control the autonomic nervous system, which is involved in the body's stress reaction. Individuals learn to engage the parasympathetic nerve system—the body's "rest and digest" mode—via breathwork, grounding exercises, and other somatic treatments, which counteracts the physiological consequences of stress and promotes relaxation.

3. Tension and Trauma Release: Somatic therapy offers a safe and supportive environment in which people may explore and release tension, trauma, and emotional blocks held in their bodies. Individuals may relieve stress and emotions by participating in gentle movement activities, body-centred awareness methods, and somatic experience exercises.

4. Emotional Regulation: Anxiety and stress are sometimes caused by difficulty in managing emotions and dealing with life's obstacles. Somatic therapy provides people with skills and practices for better emotional management. Individuals' emotional resilience and stability improve as they learn to recognize, express, and control their emotions via embodied activities.

5. Mind-Body Integration: Somatic therapy helps people notice and resolve the links between their bodily experiences, ideas, and emotions. Somatic therapy creates a feeling of coherence, alignment, and completeness by bridging the gap between the conscious and unconscious components of the self, thus minimising the fragmentation associated with anxiety and stress.

6. Improved Self-Regulation: Somatic therapy teaches patients how to control their physiological arousal, manage stress, and react adaptively to difficult circumstances. Individuals receive a feeling of mastery and control over their internal experiences as their self-awareness, self-compassion, and self-regulation abilities improve, minimising the influence of anxiety and stress on their overall well-being.

Overall, somatic therapy provides a multidimensional approach to anxiety and stress treatment, treating these problems at their root and encouraging people to create better resilience, relaxation, and well-being in their life. Somatic therapy, by using the body's intrinsic potential for healing and self-regulation, offers a road to increased freedom, energy, and mental clarity.

Chapter 2: The Effects of Trauma and Stress

When something awful occurs to you, it may have an impact on both your mind and your body. This is referred to as trauma. Trauma may result from a variety of causes, including accidents, abuse, or terrifying situations. It's like a huge jolt to the system.

Consider how terrified or hurt you could be. Your brain and body respond in various ways. Your heart may race, your muscles may tighten, and you may feel as if you are unable to breathe normally. This is all part of your body's normal reaction to danger.

However, the frightening sensations do not always subside. Chronic stress occurs when you continue to feel worried or anxious for an extended period. This might happen when you're coping with a long-term issue, such as money, family, or job stress.

Understanding Trauma: Trauma may occur in several ways. There's acute trauma, which results from a rapid and severe occurrence, such as a vehicle accident. Then there's chronic trauma, which occurs over time, such as when you're in an abusive relationship. Both sorts of trauma may have a significant influence on your emotions and behaviour.

When something terrifying occurs, your brain attempts to protect you by remembering it. However, these recollections may sometimes create issues. You may have nightmares, flashbacks, or constant anxiety. These are signals that your brain is still attempting to figure out what occurred.

Chronic tension seems like a continual weight on your shoulders. Your body remains on high alert, ready to cope with whatever comes your way.

However, this might have a negative impact on your health.

When you're anxious, your body produces substances such as cortisol and adrenaline. These may be beneficial in the short term, but chronic stress can be harmful to your health. It may cause high blood pressure, decreased immune systems, and difficulty sleeping.

Trauma impacts not just the psyche but also the physical body. Even when your mind wants to forget what occurred, your body remembers. This might manifest as bodily symptoms such as headaches, stomachaches, and muscular tightness.

The polyvagal hypothesis describes how trauma affects your body. It's like your body's alarm system is out of sync. Your nervous system goes into overdrive, leaving you uneasy, worried, or shutting down.

Coping with Trauma and Stress: While dealing with trauma and stress may be challenging, there are effective coping strategies. Building resilience is analogous to arming your mind and body to face adversity. It's about developing good coping mechanisms and recovering from setbacks.

Self-care is really essential. This includes getting adequate sleep, eating nutritious meals, and engaging in activities that make you happy. Support from friends, family, or a therapist may also be quite beneficial.

Examining Trauma and Stress Responses

When something really frightening or distressing occurs, your body and mind respond in distinct ways. This is referred to as the stress reaction. It's like your body's attempt to shield you from harm. However, when you go through really difficult situations, such as accidents or abuse, it might lead to trauma. Trauma is like a powerful jolt to your system, influencing how you feel and behave.

Understanding the Stress Response: Imagine travelling in the woods and seeing a bear. Your heart begins hammering, your muscles tighten, and you may feel unable to move. This is how your body prepares to cope with danger. It's referred to as the fight-or-flight reaction.

To help you respond rapidly, your body produces substances such as adrenaline and cortisol. This may be useful in brief periods, such as when you need to flee from a bear. However, prolonged stress may be hazardous to your health.

Recognizing Trauma: Trauma is caused by a negative experience, such as a vehicle accident or a frightening incident. It has the potential to have long-term consequences for both your mind and body. You could have nightmares, flashbacks, or constant anxiety. These are signals that your body is still attempting to digest what occurred.

Chronic stress is like carrying a big load on your shoulders all the time. It might stem from long-term challenges such as financial difficulties or familial issues. Constant stress may tire you out and make it difficult to deal with regular life.

Coping with Trauma and Stress: While dealing with trauma and chronic stress may be challenging, there are ways to improve your well-being. Taking care of your body by getting adequate sleep, eating nutritious meals, and exercising may have a significant impact. Finding assistance from friends, family, or a therapist may also help you get through difficult times.

Remember that it is quite OK to seek assistance when necessary. You don't have to face difficult situations alone. With time and assistance, it is possible to recover from trauma and learn good stress management techniques.

The impact of trauma on the body and nervous system

When you experience anything really frightening or unpleasant, such as an accident or abuse, it may have a significant influence on your body and how it functions. This is referred to as trauma. Trauma may have an impact on your nervous system, which serves as your body's control centre for how you think, feel, and respond to situations.

- Understanding Your Body's Response to Trauma:

When confronted with danger, your body goes into overdrive to defend you. It's like turning a switch that activates your fight-or-flight reaction. Your heart beats quicker, your muscles tighten, and your senses sharpen. This allows you to respond swiftly and hence survive.

However, when you are traumatised, your body may get locked in this state of heightened alert. It's as if your nervous system is unable to turn off the danger signal, even after the threat has passed. This may lead to a variety of physical and mental disorders.

Trauma may cause physical symptoms, in addition to mental ones. You could always feel strained, achy, or fatigued. You may get stomach pain or more frequent headaches. These bodily signs are your body's method of indicating that something is wrong.

Trauma may affect your neurological system in several ways. It might make you feel nervous, apprehensive, or always on edge. This is because your stress response system is out of balance. Your brain produces substances such as adrenaline and cortisol, which may keep you on high alert.

Trauma may also cause you to feel numb or alienated from your own body. It's as if your nervous system shuts down to save you from experiencing too much pain. However, this might make it difficult to communicate with people and enjoy life.

- **Coping with Trauma:** While dealing with trauma may be challenging, there are steps you can take to improve your well-being. Taking care of your body by getting adequate sleep, eating good meals, and exercising might assist to relax your nervous system. Finding assistance from friends, family, or a therapist may also help you cope with trauma and feel secure again.

Remember that recovering from trauma requires time and patience. It is important to be nice to yourself and give yourself permission to seek assistance when needed. With assistance and self-care, you may recover from trauma and find peace in your body and mind.

Understanding Chronic Stress and Its Effects

Chronic stress occurs when you experience stress over an extended period of time, such as while coping with recurring difficulties or anxieties. It's like carrying a big weight on your shoulders that refuses to go away. Chronic stress may have a variety of effects on your body and mind, and understanding the implications is critical.

Chronic stress causes your body to produce substances such as cortisol and adrenaline to assist you cope. These molecules offer you a surge of energy and allow you to respond rapidly to danger. However, prolonged stress may be hazardous to your health. Your body maintains a state of heightened alert, which may tire you out over time.

Chronic stress may have physical consequences for your body. It may cause high blood pressure, heart disease, and a compromised immune system. You may also have headaches, muscular tightness, or stomachaches. These bodily signs indicate that your body is having difficulty dealing with stress.

Stress may have mental and emotional effects, in addition to physical symptoms. You could constantly feel worried, angry, or overwhelmed. Chronic stress might make it difficult to focus, sleep, or enjoy activities you used to love. If left untreated, it may cause mental health issues such as sadness or anxiety.

Chronic stress may negatively impact your health and well-being in the long run. It may raise your chances of acquiring chronic illnesses such as diabetes, obesity, and some forms of cancer. It may also make it more difficult for you to deal with other issues in your life, such as job or relationships.

Coping with Chronic Stress: While dealing with chronic stress may be challenging, there are steps you can do to improve your mood. Taking care of your body by getting adequate rest, eating nutritious meals, and exercising on a regular basis will help you minimise stress. Finding strategies to unwind and relax, such as mindfulness or spending time in nature, may also make a significant impact. Also, if you're having trouble dealing with chronic stress on your own, don't be reluctant to seek help from friends, family, or therapists. Remember that you don't have to cope with it alone; there are individuals who can assist you in finding strategies to manage stress and enhance your overall well-being.

Chapter 3: Foundations of Somatic Healing

Somatic healing is a comprehensive approach to wellbeing that acknowledges the interdependence of the mind, body, and spirit. It is founded on the belief that our bodies contain significant knowledge and information about our emotional experiences and psychological well-being. Somatic healing tries to increase total well-being by focusing on physical sensations, movements, and emotions.

Somatic healing involves connecting with one's body and listening to its signals. It's similar to tuning into a radio station to improve your listening experience. By paying attention to our body sensations, motions, and feelings, we may learn a lot about ourselves and what we need to recover.

Somatic healing acknowledges the mind-body connection. When we go through difficult moments, such as accidents or abuse, our bodies might remember the events for a long time. This might manifest as bodily symptoms such as stress, discomfort, or weariness. Working with our body allows us to release these trapped emotions and feel better.

Somatic healing is a gentle and loving method to dealing with trauma. Somatic therapists help clients experience their emotions in their bodies rather than just discussing what occurred. This may assist to release pent-up energy and emotions, allowing for deeper healing.

Somatic healing involves several practical strategies. Breathing exercises, movement therapy, and body-centred awareness techniques are just a few examples. These approaches help clients become more aware of their bodies and how they feel, allowing them to work through their problems in a safe and supportive environment.

Somatic healing provides relief from physical pain, mental discomfort, and prior traumas. Somatic therapy, which utilises the body's inherent healing mechanisms, may help decrease stress, enhance mood, and increase general well-being. It may also help you gain self-awareness, resilience, and improve your relationships.

Body Awareness and Sensations

Body awareness refers to paying attention to what your body is telling you. It's like listening to your body's signals and messages to figure out how you're feeling and what you need. Sensations are bodily experiences such as warmth, tingling, or stress. Developing body awareness entails being more sensitive to these feelings and learning how to interpret them.

Body awareness involves conversing with one's own body. Listen to what it's saying and answer with care and attention. When you are aware of your body, you notice things like how stiff your muscles are or the feeling of your breath moving in and out of your body. This awareness allows you to connect with yourself on a deeper level and may lead you in making decisions that promote your well-being.

Sensations are the bodily sensations you sense in your body. They may feel pleasant, such as the warmth of sunlight on your skin, or unpleasant, such as the tightness in your chest when you're nervous. Paying attention to sensations may provide you with useful information about your mental state and help you understand how your body reacts to various circumstances.

Developing bodily awareness improves general health and well-being. It may help you cope with stress and anxiety by bringing you into the present moment and anchoring you in your body. It may also help improve your posture and movement patterns, resulting in greater physical health and a lower chance of injury. Furthermore, bodily awareness may improve your emotional intelligence and interpersonal interactions by allowing you to detect and express your emotions more effectively.

Practical Techniques: There are several techniques to improve body awareness in everyday life. Mindfulness exercises, such as body scans and mindful breathing, may help you tune into your body's feelings and become more present in the moment. Movement techniques such as yoga or tai chi may also help you gain body awareness by pushing you to move with purpose and pay attention to how your body feels as you go through various positions or sequences.

Techniques for breathing and anchoring

Effective strategies for stress management, mind-calming, and staying in the present moment include breathwork and grounding exercises. In order to develop a feeling of inner stability, calm, and relaxation, these techniques use the breath and deliberate movements.

Methods for Breathwork:

1. Diaphragmatic Breathing: In order to expand the diaphragm muscle, which is situated behind the lungs, one must take deep breaths. This technique is also referred to as belly breathing. Choose a comfortable sitting or sleeping posture to begin practising diaphragmatic breathing. Grasp your belly with one hand and your chest with the other. As you fill your lungs with oxygen, take a deep breath through your nose and feel your belly rise. Next, gently release the breath via your mouth while seeing your belly drop. Pay attention to the way your breath enters and exits your body. By encouraging calmness and lowering tension, diaphragmatic breathing aids in triggering the body's relaxation response.

2. Box Breathing: Box breathing is a basic method that includes breathing in a regulated sequence. For box breathing exercises, take a deep breath through your nose, hold it for four counts, release it gently through your mouth for four counts, and then hold it once again for four counts. Several times over, repeat this process while paying attention to the rhythmic cycle of inhalation, retention, expiration, and pause. Box breathing helps lessen anxiety, help the neurological system function properly, and increase attention and focus.

3. Dr. Andrew Weil's 4-7-8 breathing method is a soothing breathing practice that promotes stress relief and relaxation. First, choose a comfortable position to sit or lie in to begin practising 4-7-8 breathing. When you count to four, close your eyes and inhale deeply through your nose. Take a seven-count breath hold. Then, for a count of eight, gently and fully exhale through your mouth while whooshing. Three more times through this cycle, concentrate on feeling relaxed with each breath. For the purpose of encouraging sleep and easing stress, 4-7-8 breathing might be very useful.

Methods of Grounding:

1. Mindfulness of the Body: This practice entails raising your consciousness to the bodily sensations that are inside you. Locate a calm area where you are able to stand or sit comfortably. To focus yourself, close your eyes and take several deep breaths. Next, take a calm, thorough look over your whole body, noting any pressure, tingling, or warmth that you may experience. Consider focusing on the feel of your feet hitting the ground or the in and out motion of your breath. Anxiety and a sense of overwhelm may be diminished by anchoring yourself in the here and now and paying attention to your body's sensations.

2. Visualisation: Visualisation methods help you feel stable and grounded by using your imagination. Locate a peaceful area where you may unwind and sit comfortably. To focus yourself, close your eyes and take several deep breaths. Next, see a brilliant, shielding light enveloping you. Imagine that the soles of your feet are roots that go deep into the ground, securing you to the spot. Imagine feeling safe and protected as you are a part of the earth's energy. Another option is to picture oneself in a serene natural environment, like a beach or forest, and let the sights, sounds, and feelings of the environment bring you back to the present. You may instil a feeling of stability and security in yourself by using your imagination in this manner.

3. Physical Activity: Taking little, modest physical exercises might help you to centre yourself and alleviate stress in your body. Locate a cosy spot with plenty of room to walk about, such a peaceful room or a patio. To start, focus yourself by inhaling deeply a few times. Then do some basic exercises that help you feel connected to your body and the ground. Some examples of these exercises include stretching your body gently, doing tai chi or yoga, or going for barefoot walks on grass or sand. Feel the sense of movement in your body and the connection you have with the ground under your feet. You can let go of stored energy and encourage serenity and relaxation by moving deliberately and mindfully.

You may improve your feeling of wellbeing, manage stress, and lessen anxiety by implementing these grounding and breathwork practices into your everyday routine. Try out several techniques until you discover the one that suits you the best. Always remember to approach your practice with patience, curiosity, and self-compassion. You may develop a stronger bond with your body, mind, and spirit over time with steady work, which will make it easier and more resilient for you to deal with life's obstacles.

Expressive Gratitude in Somatic Orientation

Somatic therapy, a holistic approach to healing that stresses the interdependence of the mind, body, and spirit, is based on movement and expression. Within the context of somatic therapy, the body's accumulated emotional, psychological, and physical stress may be explored, processed, and released with the use of movement and expressive arts.

- Knowing Movement in Somatic Therapy: Movement is essential to somatic therapy because it allows patients to establish a stronger connection with their bodies and to reach deeply layered levels of awareness and comprehension. Clients are able to relieve tension and reestablish inner balance by exploring memories, emotions, and sensations that are stored inside the body via deliberate movement techniques. To promote embodiment, self-expression, and holistic healing, movement modalities including dance, yoga, qigong, and tai chi are often included into somatic therapy sessions.

- Examining Expression in Somatic Therapy: The external expression of one's inner feelings, ideas, and experiences is referred to as expression. Verbal communication, creative expression, and nonverbal body language are all examples of expression in somatic therapy. In order to facilitate the investigation and processing of feelings and experiences that may be difficult to articulate, clients are urged to express themselves honestly and without fear of criticism. Through expressive activities, such as role-playing, writing, sketching, or dancing, clients may develop a stronger feeling of agency and empowerment as well as a deeper understanding of their inner selves.

- Movement and Expression in Somatic Therapy: Including movement and expression in somatic therapy has many advantages for those looking for holistic healing and personal development.

Enables clients to move beyond and integrate unresolved emotions and prior traumas by facilitating emotional release and processing.

- Promotes self-healing and a closer relationship with oneself by raising somatic intelligence and body awareness.
- By inducing the body's relaxation response and calming the neurological system, it facilitates relaxation, stress reduction, and emotional management.
- Strengthens communication, self-expression, and creative abilities by giving people new ways to communicate their inner needs and experiences.

Encourages comprehensive healing and change on many levels of existence by supporting the integration of mind, body, and spirit.

People may access the body's inherent knowledge and healing capacity by embracing movement and expression in the framework of somatic therapy, which promotes increased self-awareness, resilience, and general well-being. Movement and expression are potent catalysts for healing, development, and change in somatic therapy, whether they are used via body-centred psychotherapy approaches, expressive arts therapy, or mindful movement practices.

Chapter 4:Interventions using Somatics to Reduce Anxiety

Chronic worry, fear, or uneasiness are prevalent mental health concerns that are often accompanied by physical symptoms including tension, restlessness, and trouble focusing. Anxiety may also take the form of any of these feelings. As difficult as it might be to control anxiety, somatic approaches provide useful methods for easing symptoms, encouraging calmness, and regaining equilibrium.

The Knowledge of Somatic Methods:

As physical sensations, emotions, and ideas are interrelated, somatic therapies emphasise this relationship between the mind and body. Through mindful activities that encourage relaxation and overall well being, these strategies seek to reduce stress, heighten bodily awareness, and balance the nervous system.

Exhalation:

Controlling and regulating one's breath consciously is the core of breathwork, a basic somatic method for relieving anxiety. People may elicit the relaxation response in their bodies, which calms the nervous system and lessens feelings of tension and anxiety, by taking deeper, slower breaths. In order to induce calm and reestablish equilibrium, breathwork practitioners often use techniques including diaphragmatic breathing, box breathing, and 4-7-8 breathing.

Scan of the Body:

By methodically bringing awareness to various bodily areas, observing sensations, and letting go of tension, one may practise mindfulness called a "body scan." Focusing on every part of the body, from head to toe, and noting any feelings, such tightness, tingling, or warmth, is the instruction given to participants during a body scan. In this manner, people may become more aware of their bodies, which helps them relax, release tension from their muscles, and feel peaceful and in good health.

Empathy-Building and Stress-Reduction Activities

Exercises for grounding people in the present make them feel more stable, focused, and at ease. They are useful methods for fostering these characteristics. Those who use these exercises will be able to anchor themselves in the present now and reduce emotions of overload, tension, or worry by anchoring themselves in their bodies and surroundings.

Understanding Activities for Grounding:

With a focus on the value of the mind-body connection and the potency of present-moment awareness, grounding exercises are based on the ideas of mindfulness and somatic therapy. With the use of these sensory-engaging activities and a concentration on bodily sensations, people may learn to move their attention from racing thoughts to the calm and steady present moment.

Techniques for Grounding:

1. The First Thing to Consider: The goal of this exercise is to become aware of the bodily sensations that are experienced, such as the sensation of your hands resting on your lap, your feet hitting the floor, or the movement of your breath in and out of your body. People may de-stress and reduce feelings of overload by concentrating on these experiences. This helps them to stay rooted in the present.

2. Technical Details: 5-4-3-2-1 Using the senses, this practice fosters a feeling of grounding and helps people connect with their environment. The 5-4-3-2-1 approach asks participants to list and identify five objects they can see, four objects they can touch, three objects they can hear, two objects they can smell, and one object they can taste. With the use of this practice, people may learn to refocus their attention from worrying thoughts to the cosy and tranquil present moment.

3. Rooting Diagram: People are asked to see themselves as trees with deeply ingrained roots in the ground as part of this practice. Feeling rooted and supported in their environment, they see themselves taking power and stability from the soil underneath them. By encouraging emotions of peace and centering, this vision aids people in developing a sense of stability and security.

4. Soliciting Verses: Reciting positive sentences to oneself might help people feel more stable and at ease. This technique is known as grounding affirmation. **"I am rooted and grounded in the**

present moment," "I feel secure and safe in my surroundings," and "I trust in my ability to handle whatever comes my way" are a few examples of grounding affirmations. People may strengthen sentiments of resilience and centre themselves by repeating these affirmations. Grounding exercises provide many advantages.

Enhances resilience and coping mechanisms for handling challenging emotions or circumstances. Promotes relaxation and stress reduction. Raises awareness and mindfulness in the present moment. Reduces feelings of anxiety, overwhelm, or dissociation.

Progressive Muscular Relaxation (PMR):

Progressive muscle relaxation is a method that includes tensing and then relaxing various muscular groups in the body, so progressively decreasing tension and encouraging relaxation. Individuals begin by tensing a certain muscular region, such as their shoulders or fists, for a few seconds before gradually releasing the tension and concentrating on the feelings of relaxation. Individuals who practise PMR on a daily basis may learn to notice and release muscular tension, decrease anxiety-related physical symptoms, and enhance general relaxation and well-being.

Mindful movement:

Mindful movement activities, including yoga, tai chi, and qigong, integrate gentle, focused movements with breath awareness and mindfulness. These techniques encourage relaxation, develop bodily awareness, and allow people to connect with the present moment. Individuals who move thoughtfully and with a goal may relieve physical stress, quiet the mind, and build a feeling of inner peace and tranquillity.

Visualisation:

Visualisation is a method that uses the imagination to generate peaceful mental pictures or situations. Individuals might envision themselves in a quiet, serene setting, such as a beach or forest, or overcome obstacles with confidence and ease. Individuals may use their imagination to move their attention away from unpleasant thoughts and sensations, increasing relaxation and lessening feelings of stress and anxiety.

The advantages of somatic techniques for anxiety relief:

- Promotes relaxation and stress reduction
- Reduces anxiety symptoms including muscular tightness and fast heartbeat
- Enhances body awareness and mindfulness
- Gives a feeling of control and empowerment over anxious symptoms
- Develops resilience and coping abilities to manage anxiety in everyday life.

Breathwork Techniques for Nervous System Regulation

Breathwork methods have a dramatic influence on the neural system, facilitating relaxation, stress reduction, and general well-being. Individuals may control the autonomic nervous system, which regulates automatic biological activities such as heart rate, digestion, and stress response, by deliberately modulating their breathing. In this thorough tutorial, we will look at several breathwork techniques and their implications on nervous system modulation.

Understanding the nervous system:

Before getting into breathwork routines, it's important to understand how the nervous system regulates physiological processes and responds to stress. The autonomic nervous system is divided into two branches: the sympathetic nervous system, which controls the body's fight-or-flight reaction to perceived threats, and the parasympathetic nervous system, which promotes relaxation and equilibrium after a stressful event.

Breathing Techniques for Nervous System Regulation:

1. Diaphragmatic Breathing: Deep inhalations activate the diaphragm muscle, causing a gradual and constant expansion of the abdomen. This approach activates the vagus nerve, a vital component of the parasympathetic nervous system, which promotes relaxation and reduces stress. To conduct diaphragmatic breathing, lay down or sit comfortably, put one hand on your lower abdomen and the other on your upper body, and inhale deeply through your nose, letting your belly rise. Exhale gently through your lips, feeling your stomach drop. Repeat this technique for a few minutes, concentrating on the rhythm of your breath and the feelings in your body.

2. Box Breathing: This simple but effective method calms the nervous system and promotes relaxation. This exercise consists of breathing, holding, expelling, and holding the breath at equal intervals, resulting in a repetitive pattern resembling the sides of a square. Individuals who regulate their breathing in this manner might stimulate the body's relaxation response, reducing feelings of worry and tension. To practise box breathing, inhale deeply through your nose for four counts, hold your breath for four counts, exhale gently through your mouth for four counts, and then hold your breath for another four counts. Repeat this cycle multiple times, letting your body and mind relax with each inhalation.

3. Alternate Nostril Breathing: This yogic breathing practice, also known as Nadi Shodhana or Anulom Vilom, balances the left and right hemispheres of the brain and promotes calm. This exercise entails alternating the passage of air between the left and right nostrils, with the fingers blocking one nostril at a time. Alternate nostril breathing is thought to stimulate the parasympathetic nervous system, which relaxes the mind and reduces stress. To practise alternate nostril breathing, sit comfortably with your spine straight and seal your right nostril with your right thumb. Inhale deeply through your left nostril, then close your left nostril with your right ring finger and exhale through your right nose. Inhale via your right nostril, then shut it with your thumb and breathe out through your left nose. Continue this cycle for many minutes, paying attention to your breathing and body sensations.

Advantages of Breathwork for Nervous System Regulation:

- Promotes relaxation and stress reduction
- Balances the autonomic nervous system
- Improves mental clarity and focus
- Enhances emotional control and resilience
- Supports general well-being and vitality

Progressive Muscle Relaxation Techniques.

Progressive Muscle Relaxation (PMR) is a well-known and efficient relaxation method that includes contracting and then releasing various muscle groups in the body. PMR, invented by American physician Edmund Jacobson in the early twentieth century, is commonly used to relieve stress, muscular tension, and enhance general relaxation. In this complete tutorial, we will look at the concepts of PMR, how to use them, and the multiple advantages it has for both physical and mental health.

Understanding progressive muscle relaxation:

PMR is founded on the idea that muscular tension and mental stress are inextricably linked, and that learning to release tension in the body may lead to a decrease in psychological stress. The method is gradually tensing certain muscle groups for a few seconds before releasing the tension, enabling the muscles to completely relax. Individuals who engage in this practice may raise their awareness of muscular tension, encourage relaxation, and achieve a feeling of serenity and well-being.

How To Practice Progressive Muscle Relaxation:

1. **Find a peaceful Space**: Start by looking for a peaceful and comfortable place to sit or lay down without being interrupted.

2. **Concentrate on Breath:** Take a few deep breaths to ground yourself and focus your attention on the present moment.

3. **Progressive Muscle Tensing:** Begin with a single muscle group, such as your hands or arms. Clench your muscles firmly and maintain the tension for 5-10 seconds, paying close attention to the feelings of strain.

4. Release Tension: Immediately release the tension in the muscles and allow them to fully relax. Consider the difference between the sensations of tension and relaxation.

5. Repeat with Other Muscle Groups: Move on to the next muscle group, working your way across the body. Tense and relax common muscle groups such as the shoulders, neck, face, chest, belly, buttocks, thighs, and calves.

6. Concentrate on feelings: As you tense and release each muscle group, notice the feelings of tension melting away and relaxation spreading throughout your body.

7. Practice Regularly: Aim to practise PMR for 10-20 minutes every day, progressively increasing the length as you grow more comfortable with the method.

Benefits of Progressive Muscle Relaxation:

- **Reduces tension and Anxiety**: PMR promotes relaxation and calms the neurological system, making it very helpful in lowering psychological tension and anxiety.

- **Reduces Muscle Tension:** By methodically tensing and releasing various muscle groups, PMR helps to relieve muscular tension and stiffness, minimising physical discomfort and pain.

- **Improves Sleep Quality**: Practising PMR before bedtime may help people relax and prepare for sleep, resulting in better sleep quality and duration.

- **Improves Mind-Body Awareness:** PMR raises awareness of physical sensations and the mind-body link, helping people to identify and manage indicators of stress and tension.

- **Improves Overall Well-Being:** Regular PMR practice may help to promote relaxation, reduce stress-related symptoms, and increase resistance to stressors.

Chapter 5: Exploring Mind-Body Connections

The idea of mind-body links refers to the complex interplay between our mental and physical processes. This interconnection implies that our ideas, emotions, and actions have a significant effect on our physical health, just as our bodily sensations and experiences have an impact on our mental health. In this thorough book, we will look at the complicated network of mind-body connections, how they appear in our everyday lives, and what they mean for general health and wellbeing.

Understanding the Mind-Body Connection:

The mind-body link is fundamentally based on the premise that our mental and emotional moods may have a direct influence on our physical health, and vice versa. According to research, psychological variables such as stress, anxiety, and depression may contribute to the onset or worsening of physical health issues such as cardiovascular disease, digestive disorders, and chronic pain. In contrast, bodily feelings like pain, weariness, and disease may have an impact on our mood, cognition, and emotional well-being.

The role of stress:

Stress is one of the most important variables in mind-body interactions. When we are stressed, whether from external causes like job or relationships, or internal factors like unpleasant thoughts or emotions, our bodies activate the sympathetic nervous system, often known as the "fight-or-flight" reaction. This physiological reaction causes a series of changes in the body, including increased heart rate, high blood pressure, and raised levels of stress chemicals like cortisol and adrenaline. Chronic stress has been related to a variety of physical and mental health issues, such as heart disease, immunological malfunction, digestive disorders, anxiety, and depression.

Emotional and Physical Health:

Our emotions play an important role in mind-body relationships. Happiness, appreciation, and love have been demonstrated in studies to have a good impact on physical health, encouraging cardiovascular health, boosting immunological function, and improving general well-being. Negative emotions, such as anger, grief, and fear, may contribute to the formation or worsening of physical health issues, raising the risk of chronic illnesses and impairing immunological function.

Practical applications:

Understanding the mind-body link has significant implications for health and wellness practices.

Meditation, yoga, tai chi, and mindfulness-based stress reduction have all been found to help people relax, decrease stress, and enhance their physical and mental health. These activities highlight the significance of raising awareness of the mind-body link, encouraging self-care behaviours, and advocating for holistic approaches to health and healing.

Implementing Mind-Body Practices:

Incorporating mind-body activities into everyday life may help people develop a better understanding of the mind-body link while also promoting general health and wellbeing. These practices might include mindfulness meditation, deep breathing exercises, progressive muscle relaxation, expressive arts therapy, or mind-body movements like yoga or tai chi. Individuals who cultivate the mind-body connection via regular practice may increase their resistance to stress, improve relaxation, and build a stronger feeling of balance and harmony in their life.

Mindfulness Meditation for Stress Reduction.

In today's fast-paced world, stress has become an accepted part of everyday life, affecting our physical health, emotional well-being, and general quality of life. Fortunately, mindfulness meditation provides a simple yet effective approach for stress reduction and relaxation. In this thorough introduction, we will look at the fundamentals of mindfulness meditation, how to practise it successfully, and the myriad advantages it provides for stress relief and general well-being.

Understanding Mindful Meditation:

Mindfulness meditation is a technique for bringing focused attention to the present moment without judgement or attachment to ideas, emotions, or sensations. Mindfulness meditation, which has its roots in ancient contemplative traditions like Buddhism, has grown in popularity in recent years as a secular practice for encouraging relaxation, lowering stress, and improving general well-being. Mindfulness allows people to become more aware of their internal and external experiences, promoting a feeling of peace, clarity, and presence.

How to practise mindfulness meditation:

1. Find a peaceful Space: Start by looking for a peaceful and comfortable place to sit or lay down without being interrupted.

2. Maintain a Comfortable Posture: Sit comfortably and erect, with your spine straight and your hands softly resting on your lap or legs. Alternatively, you may lay on your back, arms at your sides and legs gently stretched.

3. Concentrate on Your Breath: Close your eyes and pay attention to your breath. Feel the experience of the breath as it enters and exits your body without attempting to control or influence it.

4. Develop Nonjudgmental Awareness: As you continue to concentrate on your breathing, ideas, emotions, and sensations may occur. Instead of being immersed in these sensations, just watch them with curiosity and compassion, allowing them to pass without judgement.

5. Return to the Breath: When you sense your mind straying or getting distracted, gently bring your focus back to the breath, which serves as an anchor to the present moment.

6. Practice Regularly: Aim for 10-20 minutes of mindfulness meditation every day, gradually increasing the length as you get more comfortable with the practice.

Advantages of Mindfulness Meditation for Stress Reduction:

- **Promotes Relaxation**: Mindfulness meditation triggers the body's relaxation response, which reduces stress hormones like cortisol and promotes sensations of peace and quiet.

- **Improves Emotional Regulation:** By fostering awareness of thoughts, feelings, and sensations, mindfulness meditation assists people in developing stronger emotional resilience and regulation, minimising reaction to stress.

- **Improves Focus and Concentration**: Regular mindfulness meditation practice improves attentional control and cognitive flexibility, helping people to concentrate on tasks and activities without becoming overwhelmed by stress.

- **Increases Self-Awareness:** Mindfulness meditation promotes self-awareness and introspection, allowing people to identify and address causes of stress and tension in their daily life.

- **Promotes Overall Well-Being:** In addition to stress reduction, mindfulness meditation has been linked to a variety of health and well-being advantages, including better sleep quality, improved immune function, and increased life satisfaction.

Body Scanning and Sensory Awareness Activities

Body scanning and sensory awareness exercises are mindfulness techniques that entail paying close attention to various sensations and locations of the body. These activities encourage relaxation, self-awareness, and present-moment awareness, making them useful tools for stress reduction and general well-being. In this complete book, we will look at the fundamentals of body scanning and sensory awareness exercises, as well as how to use them successfully and reap the myriad advantages for mind-body wellness.

Understanding body scanning and sensory awareness:

Body scanning is a mindfulness technique that entails deliberately focusing attention on various regions of the body, recognizing sensations, and increasing awareness of the present moment. Individuals may improve their self-awareness and calmness by scanning their whole body from head to toe. Sensory awareness exercises entail concentrating attention on the five senses—sight, hearing, touch, taste, and smell—in order to increase present-moment awareness and relaxation.

How to Improve Body Scanning and Sensory Awareness:

1. Find a Comfortable Position: Start by locating a comfortable and peaceful place to sit or lay down without being distracted.

2. Close Your Eyes: Take a few deep breaths to calm yourself and focus your attention within.

3. Begin with the Feet: Focus your focus on your feet as you begin your body scanning routine. Feel for any feelings in your feet and toes, such as warmth, tingling, or pressure.

4. transfer Up the Body: Gradually transfer your focus upward, examining each portion of the body in turn. Feel feelings in your legs, hips, belly, chest, arms, hands, shoulders, neck, and head.

5. Observe Without Judgment: As you scan each portion of your body, notice any feelings that come without judgement or attachment. Simply watch them arrive and leave.

6. Sensory Awareness Exercises: In addition to body scanning, you may do sensory awareness exercises by paying attention to each of the five senses. For example, you can observe the colours and forms around you (sight), listen to the noises in your surroundings (hearing), feel the texture of things or surfaces (touch), taste and appreciate food or drink consciously (tasting), and inhale and note any fragrances or aromas.

Advantages of Body Scanning and Sensory Awareness

- Promotes Relaxation: Body scanning and sensory awareness activities increase the body's relaxation response, which reduces stress chemicals like cortisol and promotes sensations of peace and serenity.

- **Increases Self-Awareness:** By directing concentrated attention to various feelings and parts of the body, these techniques promote more self-awareness and introspection, allowing people to identify and resolve causes of stress and tension.

- Improves Mindfulness: Body scanning and sensory awareness exercises promote present-moment awareness, assisting people in being anchored in the current moment and reducing ruminating on past or future occurrences.

- Enhances Body Awareness: These techniques increase awareness of bodily sensations, establishing a stronger connection to the physical body and increasing somatic intelligence.

- Improves Emotional Regulation: By increasing awareness of physical sensations and emotions, people may better manage their emotional reactions and deal with pressures.

Emotion Regulation Strategies Through Somatic Awareness

Emotions play an important part in our lives, impacting our ideas, actions, and general well-being. However, monitoring and regulating emotions may be difficult, particularly when confronted with pressures or unfavourable circumstances. Somatic awareness, or the practice of tuning into body feelings and experiences, provides useful tools for emotion regulation and well-being. In this book, we will look at how somatic awareness may be utilised as a strong tool for emotion regulation, as well as practical techniques for implementing it into your everyday life.

Understanding Somatic Awareness:

Somatic awareness entails paying attention to physical sensations, emotions, and experiences. This practice stresses the interdependence of mind and body, acknowledging that emotions are often expressed and felt via physical experiences. Individuals who cultivate somatic awareness may improve their comprehension of their emotional states, increase their capacity to manage emotions, and boost general emotional well-being.

Emotion Regulation Strategies using Somatic Awareness:

1. Body Scan Meditation: Body scan meditation is a mindfulness technique that entails deliberately directing attention to various regions of the body, detecting sensations, and observing any emotions that occur. Individuals may recognize regions of tension or discomfort connected with various emotions and learn to release physical tension, increasing emotional stability.

2. Breathwork: Techniques like diaphragmatic breathing and deep belly breathing may help control emotions by stimulating the body's relaxation response. Individuals who concentrate on their breathing and engage in deep, rhythmic breathing patterns may soothe their nervous system, decrease tension, and enhance sensations of relaxation and emotional stability.

3. Body Movement and Expression: Gentle body movement or expressive activities like yoga, dancing, or tai chi may help relieve tension and enhance emotional stability. These activities help people to connect with their bodies, communicate feelings nonverbally, and relieve physical stress, all of which promote emotional balance and well-being.

4. Grounding methods: Grounding methods improve emotional stability and control by drawing attention to the present moment and connecting with one's physical surroundings. Grounding exercises, sensory awareness, and visualisation may help people feel more rooted and focused, lowering anxiety and overload caused by strong emotions.

Benefits of Emotion Regulation via Somatic Awareness:

- **Increased Emotional Awareness:** Somatic awareness enables people to have a better knowledge of their emotional states and notice how they appear in the body.

- **Improved Emotional Regulation**: By paying attention to physical sensations and participating in somatic activities, people may learn to manage their emotions more effectively and deal with pressures in healthy ways.

- **Reduced Stress and Anxiety:** Somatic awareness practices enhance relaxation, lower stress levels, and relieve anxiety symptoms, all of which contribute to emotional wellbeing.

- **Increased Resilience:** By bringing somatic awareness into everyday life, people may become more resilient to stress and adversity, allowing them to traverse problems with more ease and flexibility.

Chapter 6: Combining Neuroscience and Psychology

A comprehensive approach to comprehending and treating mental health and well-being is represented by the combination of somatic practices with psychology and neuroscience. Through the integration of knowledge from other fields, professionals may enhance their understanding of the mind-body relationship and create more potent therapies aimed at fostering psychological resilience, emotional control, and general mental well-being. We will examine the integration of somatic practices with psychology and neuroscience in this guide, emphasising its importance and possible advantages for anyone looking to enhance their mental health.

Comprehending Somatic Practices:

Somatic practices are a broad category of mind-body approaches that highlight the role that bodily experiences, feelings, and movements have in fostering holistic well-being. These techniques include body scanning, yoga, tai chi, mindfulness meditation, breathwork, and other somatic modalities that support people in developing an awareness of the mind-body link and foster calmness, emotional control, and stress reduction.

Combining psychology with other fields:

Understanding the fundamental processes underlying human cognition, emotion, and behaviour is made possible by the scientific study of psychology, which focuses on the mind and behaviour. Through the incorporation of psychological ideas and concepts into somatic practices, practitioners may optimise the efficacy of somatic therapies in the treatment of mental health issues. Somatic awareness exercises and cognitive-behavioural techniques, for instance, can be used to help people recognize and confront harmful thought patterns, and acceptance and commitment therapy (ACT) and mindfulness exercises can be combined to support psychological flexibility and resilience.

Combining Neuroscience and Integration:

Understanding the neurological processes underpinning human behaviour, emotion, and cognition is possible via the study of the nervous system and brain function, or neuroscience. Practitioners may better understand how somatic practices affect brain structure and function, as well as neurological networks linked to stress, emotion management, and well-being, by fusing somatic practices with neuroscience. According to neuroimaging research, mindfulness meditation, for instance, may alter the structure and function of the brain. It has been found to enhance grey matter density in areas linked to emotion regulation and reduce activity in the amygdala, the brain's fear centre.

Advantages of Integration

- **Improved Treatment Results:** By combining somatic practices with psychology and neuroscience, mental health issues like anxiety, depression, trauma, and chronic stress may be addressed with more thorough and efficient treatment plans.

- **Holistic Well-Being**: Integration addresses the physical, psychological, and emotional components of health in order to achieve holistic well-being, which is based on the mind-body link.

- **Deeper Understanding:** Integration promotes a better comprehension of the interactions between bodily sensations, brain systems, and psychological processes, which results in more complex and successful treatments.

- **Empowerment:** People may gain more self-awareness, resilience, and agency in managing their mental health and well-being by integrating somatic activities into treatment and self-care routines.

- **Prevention:** Including somatic activities in an individual's routine may also benefit preventatively by assisting them in developing stress tolerance, overcoming hardship, and long-term maintenance of their mental and physical well-being.

Recognizing the Link Between the Brain and Body

The complex interaction between the central nervous system, which is made up of the brain and spinal cord, and the peripheral nervous system, which is made up of the nerves outside the brain and spinal cord, that controls behaviour, emotions, and physical processes is known as the "brain-body connection." This link demonstrates the reciprocal communication that occurs between the brain and the body, each of which has a significant impact on the other. The principles of the brain-body link, its importance for general health and wellbeing, and its usefulness for improving both physical and mental health will all be covered in this handbook.

The Brain-Body Connection's Anatomy:

A sophisticated web of neuronal channels that carry information between the brain and the body facilitates the brain-body connection. The brain and spinal cord make up the central nervous system, which acts as the brain's command centre. It processes sensory data, plans motor reactions, and controls essential processes including breathing, hormone release, digestion, and heart rate. Sensation, reflexes, and voluntary and involuntary movements are all made possible by the peripheral nervous system, which consists of sensory and motor nerves that transmit messages from the central nervous system to the rest of the body.

Importance for Physical and Mental Welfare:

The capacity of the body to maintain internal stability and balance in the face of external changes is known as homeostasis, and it is largely dependent on the brain-body connection. Numerous physical and mental health issues, such as persistent stress, heart disease, gastrointestinal diseases, immunological dysfunction, anxiety, depression, and chronic pain, may be brought on by dysregulation of the brain-body link. On the other hand, fostering a positive brain-body connection by lifestyle choices like consistent exercise, a nutritious diet, enough sleep, stress reduction, and social support may improve general health and wellbeing.

Relevance in Real-World Health Promotion:

Gaining an understanding of the relationship between the brain and body may help to improve both mental and physical health. Activities like breathwork, yoga, tai chi, and mindfulness meditation may help people relax, lower their stress levels, and develop a greater awareness of their bodies. These techniques have been shown to enhance mental and physical health outcomes by modifying activity in brain areas linked to emotion control, pain perception, and stress response. Furthermore, a strong brain-body connection and improved general well-being may be achieved by adopting lifestyle variables that support brain health, such as consistent physical exercise, a nutritious diet, enough sleep, social interaction, and cognitive stimulation.

The role of neuroplasticity in healing trauma

Neuroplasticity, or the brain's unique capacity to rearrange and change in response to events, is critical in the healing process for trauma survivors.

Trauma, whether physical, emotional, or psychological in nature, may have serious consequences for the brain, affecting neuronal circuits involved in emotion regulation, memory processing, and stress response. Understanding how neuroplasticity helps trauma recovery may lead to more successful therapeutic methods and treatments. In this tutorial, we will look at neuroplasticity's function in trauma healing, as well as its mechanics and practical applications.

Understanding Neuroplasticity.

Neuroplasticity is the brain's capacity to change its structure and function in response to experiences, environmental stimuli, and learning. This dynamic process includes changes in synaptic connections, the production of new neurons (neurogenesis), and the pruning of redundant or inefficient connections. Neuroplasticity occurs across the lifetime, affecting brain growth in infancy and adolescence while also enabling learning, memory, and healing from injury or trauma in maturity.

Effects of Trauma on the Brain:

Trauma may impair normal brain function and change neuronal circuits that process and regulate emotions, memories, and stress responses. For example, persistent stress or trauma may disrupt the hypothalamic-pituitary-adrenal (HPA) axis, resulting in prolonged activation of stress hormones like cortisol. This imbalance may impair cognitive performance, undermine emotional control, and raise the risk of mental health problems including anxiety, sadness, and post-traumatic stress disorder (PTSD).

Healing Trauma with Neuroplasticity:

Despite trauma's negative effects on the brain, neuroplasticity provides hope for rehabilitation and healing. Individuals may promote healing and resilience by using focused treatments and therapy techniques that tap into the brain's ability to adapt and change. The key concepts of trauma-informed care and neuroplasticity-based therapies are as follows:

1. Safety and Stability: Creating a secure and supportive environment is critical for encouraging neuroplasticity and healing trauma. Creating a feeling of safety enables people to relax, decrease hyperarousal, and participate in therapeutic activities more successfully.

2. Mindfulness and Awareness: Mindfulness techniques like meditation, deep breathing, and body scanning encourage neuroplasticity by increasing self-awareness, decreasing reaction to stimuli, and encouraging emotional control. Mindfulness-based therapies have been demonstrated to influence brain circuits involved in stress response, emotion regulation, and self-awareness, resulting in better mental health outcomes for trauma survivors.

3. Therapeutic connections: Positive therapeutic connections provide trauma survivors a safe and affirming setting in which to process their experiences, regulate emotions, and develop resilience. Therapists may help clients develop neuroplasticity by instilling trust, empathy, and cooperation, enabling them to examine and reinterpret their trauma stories.

4. Exposure and Processing: Gradual exposure to trauma-related memories, thoughts, and sensations, along with cognitive-behavioural approaches, increases neuroplasticity by allowing memory reconsolidation and desensitisation. This approach enables people to integrate fragmented memories, recast negative attitudes, and create adaptive coping methods.

5. Holistic techniques: Integrative techniques that address the mind, body, and spirit foster neuroplasticity and healing by recognizing the interdependence of physical, emotional, and psychological variables. Yoga, tai chi, expressive arts therapy, and somatic experiencing use the body's intrinsic healing power to aid the integration of traumatic events.

Integrating Somatic Approaches with Cognitive Behavioral Therapy

The combination of somatic techniques with cognitive-behavioural therapy (CBT) is an effective and comprehensive method to resolving mental health issues. While cognitive behavioural therapy (CBT) focuses on identifying and modifying harmful thinking patterns and behaviours, somatic therapies stress the role of physical sensations, movements, and experiences in promoting healing and wellbeing. By integrating these two therapy methods, practitioners may provide clients with a holistic treatment plan that addresses both the cognitive and somatic components of their experiences. In this book, we will look at the concepts of combining somatic techniques with CBT, as well as the advantages and practical consequences for clinical practice.

Understanding somatic approaches:

Somatic methods are a collection of mind-body practices that highlight the significance of physical experiences in fostering overall well-being. These treatments include mindfulness practices, breathwork, body awareness exercises, movement therapies (such as yoga and tai chi), and somatic experience, which focuses on releasing physical tension and trauma stored in the body. Somatic techniques seek to help people connect with their bodies, control their nerve systems, and process emotional experiences via physical sensations and movements.

Principles of Cognitive Behavioral Therapy:

Cognitive-behavioural therapy is a well-known and evidence-based technique for treating a variety of mental health issues, including anxiety, depression, trauma, and stress-related diseases. CBT includes goal-oriented strategies including exposure therapy, behavioural activation, and relaxation training to identify and challenge negative thinking patterns (cognitive restructuring) as well as change maladaptive behaviours. CBT seeks to help people build coping skills, modify harmful habits, and enhance their overall well-being.

Benefits of Integration:

1. Comprehensive Treatment: By combining somatic methods with cognitive behavioural therapy, therapists may provide clients with a comprehensive treatment strategy that addresses both cognitive and somatic components of their experiences. This holistic approach provides a more nuanced understanding of clients' issues and encourages healing on various levels—mental, emotional, and physical.

2. Improved Emotional Regulation: Somatic techniques may supplement CBT by giving clients more skills for controlling emotions and stress. Deep breathing, gradual muscle relaxation, and body scanning techniques help clients relax, decrease physiological arousal, and raise self-awareness, making cognitive restructuring and behaviour modification simpler.

3. Increased Body Awareness: By combining somatic techniques with CBT, clients may acquire better body awareness and sensitivity to physical sensations. This enhanced awareness enables clients to perceive the link between their ideas, emotions, and physical sensations, resulting in greater understanding and self-discovery.

4. Improved Treatment results: Research indicates that combining somatic methods with CBT may enhance treatment results for a variety of mental health disorders. Therapists may improve therapy success and encourage long-term change by addressing both cognitive and somatic aspects of their clients' experiences.

Practical implications for therapeutic practice:

Therapists who integrate somatic techniques with CBT must be adaptable, innovative, and sensitive to their clients' unique needs and preferences. Therapists may include somatic approaches into CBT sessions by using guided exercises, mindfulness practices, body-centred therapies, and experiential activities. Therapists may establish a comprehensive and powerful therapy environment by adapting treatments to clients' specific needs and using somatic and cognitive-behavioural methods.

Chapter 7: Case Studies: Healing with Somatic Therapy

Case studies provide light on the usefulness of somatic therapy in fostering healing and well-being for people dealing with a variety of mental health issues. Real-life examples demonstrate how somatic techniques, which emphasise the mind-body link and physical sensations, may result in profound transformations in clients' lives. In this tutorial, we will look at numerous case studies that show how people have healed after receiving somatic therapy procedures.

Case Study #1: Anxiety and Panic Attacks

Jane, a 35-year-old woman, sought treatment for her crippling anxiety and frequent panic episodes, which had been affecting her everyday life for years. Traditional talk therapy had brought some alleviation, but Jane continued to experience overpowering sensations of anxiety and misery. Her therapist suggested somatic therapy to help her connect with her body and manage her nervous system. Jane learnt to listen into physiological sensations, release accumulated tension, and control her breath during anxious periods thanks to somatic experience sessions. Jane reported a considerable decrease in the frequency and severity of her panic episodes over time, as well as an improvement in her general well-being and resilience.

Case Study #2: Trauma Recovery

Mark, a 45-year-old man, had been traumatised as a youngster and had suffered from post-traumatic stress disorder (PTSD) for the most of his life. Traditional therapeutic procedures had brought no comfort, and Mark felt trapped in avoidance and hypervigilance. His therapist suggested somatic therapy to help him process and integrate his painful experiences. Mark eventually learnt to endure and manage his emotions via somatic experiences and body-centred therapies, as well as to release stored trauma from his body and increase his resilience. Mark noted that as he developed confidence in his ability to negotiate difficult emotions, his relationships, job performance, and general quality of life improved.

Case Study #3: Chronic Pain Management

Sarah, a 50-year-old lady, has been suffering from severe pain for years owing to a spine injury. Despite several medical treatments, including surgery and pain pills, Sarah continued to suffer with extreme pain and restricted movement. Her doctor suggested somatic therapy as an additional method of pain management. Sarah learnt to listen to her body, relieve muscle tension, and increase body awareness via somatic movement techniques like gentle yoga and Feldenkrais. Sarah found that as she grew more aware of her body's signals and requirements, her pain intensity decreased, her functional mobility increased, and she felt more empowered to manage her chronic illness.

Key themes and insights:

These case studies illustrate a number of fundamental themes and insights on the therapeutic potential of somatic therapy:

1. **Mind-Body Connection:** Somatic therapy stresses the connection between the mind and body, understanding that emotional experiences are often stored and expressed via physical sensations. Somatic therapy fosters total healing and integration by addressing clients' cognitive and somatic experiences.

2. **Regulation and Resilience:** Somatic therapy modalities, such as breathwork, body awareness exercises, and movement practices, assist clients in regulating their nervous systems, lowering physiological arousal, and developing resilience in

the face of stress and trauma. Clients may better manage anxiety, sadness, and PTSD symptoms by learning to listen to their bodies and develop self-regulation skills.

3. Empowerment and Self-Awareness: Somatic therapy encourages clients to become active participants in their healing process, resulting in increased self-awareness, agency, and autonomy. Through experiential exercises and guided interventions, clients learn to trust their bodies, listen to their inner knowledge, and make empowered decisions that benefit their well-being.

True Stories of Transformation and Growth.

Real-life tales of transformation and growth are strong examples of the human spirit's tenacity, as well as the possibility for personal change and progress. These tales showcase the transforming experiences of people who have overcome hardship, recovered from trauma, and seize new chances for development and self-discovery. In this guide, we will look at various real-life examples of change and development to demonstrate the significant influence of resilience, tenacity, and self-reflection on the human experience.

Story #1: From Addiction to Recovery

John's tale is about addiction, hardship, and ultimate salvation. For years, John struggled with drug misuse, resulting in broken relationships, legal issues, and a downward spiral into depression. However, with the help of loved ones and expert care, John went on a road to recovery. Through treatment, support groups, and a dedication to sobriety, John learned to face his previous traumas, address the underlying problems that contributed to his addiction, and rebuild his life from the ground up. Today, John is clean, flourishing, and committed to helping others overcome addiction and find hope in their darkest times.

Story 2: Finding Purpose Following Loss

Sarah's path is one of resilience and finding meaning in the midst of loss. Sarah struggled to deal with sorrow and manage life as a single mom when her husband died in a horrific accident. Despite the great sorrow and suffering, Sarah found refuge in her desire to serve others. Sarah used her own experiences to become a grief counsellor and advocate for bereaved families. Sarah found a sense of purpose and pleasure in her job, turning her sadness into a force for good in the lives of others.

Story 3: Overcoming Adversity with Perseverance

David's tale is about overcoming hardship with endurance and commitment. David was born with a physical impairment that restricted his movement, thus he encountered various problems and obstacles throughout his life. Rather than falling to despair,

David accepted his peculiarities and refused to allow his handicap define him. David achieved his goals of being a successful entrepreneur and champion for disability rights via hard work, tenacity, and a positive attitude. Today, David is prospering in his work, breaking down barriers and pushing people to embrace their individuality and follow their hobbies without boundaries.

Key themes and insights:

These real-life tales of change and progress emphasise many crucial themes and insights:

1. Resilience: Despite enormous hurdles and disappointments, each person displayed exceptional resilience in overcoming adversity and persisting through tough times.

2. Self-Reflection: Through self-reflection and introspection, these people learned about their own strengths, shortcomings, and values, resulting in personal development and change.

3. Support and Connection: Friends, family, and the community all played important roles in helping each individual's healing, development, and recovery. They were able to overcome obstacles by relying on others for support and connection.

4. Purpose and Meaning: Discovering purpose and meaning in life enabled these people to overcome their circumstances and embrace new chances for development, satisfaction, and service to the larger good.

Example of Somatic Techniques in Practice

Somatic methods are a diverse set of mind-body practices that emphasise physiological sensations, movements, and experiences to enhance healing, self-awareness, and emotional regulation. Somatic approaches, which range from breathwork to body-centred treatments, provide people with practical skills for connecting with their bodies, relieving stress, and creating a sense of wellbeing. In this tutorial, we will look at various instances of somatic methods in action, demonstrating their adaptability and usefulness in supporting overall health and recovery.

1. **Bioenergetic Exercises**: These motions and postures aim to relieve muscle tension and stimulate emotional discharge. These exercises are based on the idea that emotional experiences are stored in the body and may be released via physical activity. Exercises like shaking, jumping, and stretching help the body release pent-up energy and emotions.

2. **Sensory Integration strategies:** These strategies try to manage sensory experiences for persons who may struggle with processing information. These strategies use sensory stimuli, such as weighted

blankets, sensory bins, and textured items, to assist people manage their arousal levels and relax.

3. Body-Mind Centering (BMC): BMC is a movement therapy technique that focuses on the connection between physical and psychological systems. Practitioners employ hands-on approaches and guided movements to help people become more aware of their own internal body feelings and movement patterns. BMC may help people gain a better knowledge of how their body and mind interact and encourage more flexibility and comfort of movement.

4. Authentic Movement: This somatic exercise includes exploring inner impulses and experiences via spontaneous, nonverbal movement. Participants shut their eyes and let their bodies to move naturally, gaining access to higher levels of awareness and self-expression. Authentic movement may aid in emotional processing, self-discovery, and the integration of mind-body experiences.

5. Rolfing Structural Integration: This hands-on bodywork approach tries to realign and balance the body's structure by manipulating fascia, which surrounds muscles and organs. Rolfing, which relieves tension and limitations in the fascia, may enhance posture, movement efficiency, and general wellbeing. This approach often entails a series of sessions to treat particular points of stress and improve structural integration.

.Readers' Perspectives on "Embodied Healing"

"Embodied Healing" has struck a deep chord with readers, providing vital insights and transforming techniques to help them on their recovery journeys. Readers have shared tales of personal development, perseverance, and empowerment as they went on their own recovery journeys. Here, we look at some thoughts from people who have purchased the book and how their recovery journeys have progressed.

1. Sarah, a reader of "Embodied Healing," suffered with self-doubt and severe self-criticism for years before discovering self-compassion. Sarah started to have a more loving and accepting connection with herself after following the book's advice on fostering self-compassion and bodily awareness. Sarah learnt to listen to her body's knowledge and heed its needs by engaging in somatic practices such as body scan meditations and gentle movement exercises. Sarah's inner dialogue evolved from self-judgement to self-compassion, enabling her to accept her flaws while celebrating her innate merit.

2. **John's Recovery from Trauma:** After experiencing childhood trauma, John discovered comfort and support in "Embodied Healing." The book's investigation of somatic methods to trauma recovery spoke directly to John, who had struggled to find effective healing techniques. John proceeded

to carefully examine and process the terrible memories held in his body using the book's somatic experience exercises and mindfulness techniques. As he learned to control his nervous system and release accumulated stress, John's emotional well-being and resilience improved significantly. With each chapter, John felt more capable of reclaiming his feeling of safety, autonomy, and completeness.

3. Maria's Journey to Mind-Body Integration: Maria, a reader of "Embodied Healing," felt estranged from her body and experienced chronic tension and anxiety. Maria became interested in somatic movement techniques like yoga and breathwork after reading the book, which emphasised mind-body connection. Maria learnt to coordinate her breath with her movements, build present-moment awareness, and let go of stress in her body via these exercises. Maria had a deep feeling of calm, groundedness, and inner serenity as she became more connected to her body's sensations and rhythms. Integrating mind-body activities into her everyday life gave her strength and resilience, allowing her to face life's problems with more ease and grace.

4. Tom's Liberation from Chronic Pain: After experiencing chronic pain for years, Tom discovered hope and healing in "Embodied Healing." The book's investigation of somatic strategies for pain management provided Tom with fresh pathways of recovery after he had exhausted standard medical therapies. Tom started to relax and reframe his connection with pain by doing body scan meditations, mild movement exercises, and self-massage methods. Tom's pain intensity and functional mobility improved gradually as he learnt to listen to his body's messages and react with compassion and inquiry. Tom felt more powerful as he practised, reclaiming his vigour and living life on his own terms.

Readers of "Embodied Healing" provide insights regarding the transforming impact of somatic methods to healing. Individuals such as Sarah, John, Maria, and Tom have used the book's methods to go on journeys of self-discovery, resilience, and empowerment, recovering their intrinsic ability for healing and well-being. As more people embrace and incorporate somatic practices into their lives, their tales may encourage others to begin on their own journeys of embodied healing and change.

Chapter 8: Cultural Sensitivity and Inclusiveness in Somatic Therapy

In the field of somatic therapy, cultural awareness and inclusion are critical. This chapter discusses the significance of recognizing and appreciating cultural diversity in somatic therapy, as well as ways for creating an inclusive and culturally responsive therapeutic setting.

Cultural sensitivity in somatic therapy entails recognizing and respecting clients' cultural origins, attitudes, beliefs, and experiences. It acknowledges that people from various cultural origins may have distinct views on health, healing, and embodiment that are influenced by their cultural heritage, social identities, and lived experiences.

Somatic therapy promotes inclusivity by fostering a safe, inviting, and supportive environment for persons from diverse cultural origins, identities, and experiences. It entails aggressively confronting prejudices, preconceptions, and power dynamics that may marginalised or exclude certain groups in the therapeutic setting.

Key Considerations for Practitioners:

1. Cultural Humility: Practitioners should approach clients with cultural humility, acknowledging their own limits and prejudices and committed to continuous self-reflection, education, and progress. Practitioners may foster a collaborative therapy relationship based on mutual trust and understanding by having an open, curious, and respectful attitude.

2. Cultural Competence: Culturally competent practitioners understand their clients' cultural origins and experiences, and they are skilled at incorporating cultural factors into their therapy work. This may include adjusting physical procedures, terminology, and therapies to reflect clients' cultural values, preferences, and communication styles.

3. Intersectionality: Somatic treatment requires an understanding of how identity variables such as race, ethnicity, gender, sexuality, ability, and socioeconomic position interact. Practitioners must grasp how different aspects of identity interact and impact clients' experiences of embodiment, health, and recovery.

4. Trauma-Informed Care: Cultural sensitivity and inclusion are essential components of trauma-informed care, which recognizes the effect of systemic oppression, discrimination, and intergenerational trauma on people's mental and emotional health. Trauma-informed practitioners provide a safe and empowering atmosphere that values their clients' resilience, strengths, and cultural resources.

Practical Strategies for Cultural Sensitivity:

1. Culturally Relevant Interventions: Practitioners may use somatic treatments, rituals, or therapeutic practices that are appropriate for their clients' cultural origins and identities.

2. Language and Communication: Practitioners should utilise culturally sensitive language and communication approaches to describe their clients' experiences, taking into account their preferred terminology and phrases.

3. Community Collaboration: Working with community groups, cultural leaders, and healers may help practitioners improve their cultural competency while also facilitating clients' access to culturally particular resources and support networks.

4. Continuing Education: Practitioners must continue to receive training, supervision, and consultation on cultural competency and diversity concerns in order to improve their knowledge and abilities in delivering culturally responsive somatic therapies.

Honouring the Diversity of Trauma and Healing

Trauma is a very personal and complicated experience that may appear in a variety of ways, depending on a person's cultural background, identity, and life events. As trauma-informed care practitioners, we must understand and respect our communities' various trauma and recovery experiences. This chapter delves into the value of cultural humility, intersectionality, and inclusion in trauma treatment, as well as ways for building therapeutic environments that respect and affirm the variety of clients' experiences.

Understanding Different Trauma Experiences:

Trauma may include a broad variety of events, such as interpersonal abuse, war, natural catastrophes, structural oppression, and intergenerational trauma. These experiences are inextricably linked to elements such as race, ethnicity, gender, sexuality, ability, and financial position, influencing people's reactions to trauma and routes to recovery.

Cultural Humility and intersectionality:

Cultural humility is the realisation of one's own limits and prejudices, along with a commitment to continuous self-reflection, learning, and progress. Practitioners of trauma therapy must approach their work with humility, respecting their clients' different cultural origins and identities, as well as the intersections of identity elements that define their trauma and recovery experiences.

Inclusivity in Traumatic Therapy:

Creating inclusive and supportive trauma treatment environments entails actively confronting prejudices, stereotypes, and power dynamics that may marginalise or exclude certain groups within the therapeutic setting. This involves employing culturally sensitive terminology, including multiple viewpoints into treatment planning, and honouring clients' lived knowledge as experts in their own situations.

Strategies to Honour Diverse Experiences:

1. Culturally Responsive therapies: Trauma therapists should use culturally appropriate therapies and therapeutic techniques that are consistent with their clients' cultural origins and identities. This may include bringing traditional healing practices, rituals, and ceremonies into therapy sessions, as well as investigating how cultural narratives and beliefs influence clients' experiences of trauma and resilience.

2. Intersectional Analysis: Practitioners should use an intersectional lens to diagnose and treat trauma, acknowledging how different aspects of identity interact and impact people's experiences of trauma and recovery. This includes investigating how institutional oppression, discrimination, and marginalisation interact with personal trauma experiences to shape clients' coping mechanisms, resilience, and access to resources.

3. Community Collaboration: Working with community groups, cultural leaders, and healers may help trauma therapists improve their cultural competency while also facilitating clients' access to culturally specific resources and support networks. Collaboration with community-based groups may also assist therapists in connecting clients with culturally appropriate services and advocacy resources.

4. Self-Reflection and Continuing Education: Trauma therapists must participate in continuous self-reflection, education, and consultation to get a better knowledge of cultural competency and diversity challenges in trauma treatment. This might include attending cultural competence training, requesting supervision from a variety of viewpoints, and actively soliciting input from clients on the cultural relevance and responsiveness of therapy approaches.

Adapting Somatic Practices to Various Cultural Contexts

Somatic therapies, based on a knowledge of the mind-body link, have the ability to provide significant healing across a wide range of cultural settings. However, it is critical to remember that what is productive and culturally suitable in one setting may not always transfer effortlessly into another. This chapter discusses the significance of adapting somatic practices to different cultural settings to ensure their relevance, accessibility, and efficacy for people from various backgrounds.

Understanding cultural sensitivity:

Cultural sensitivity is understanding and respecting people' cultural ideas, values, customs, and behaviours within a given cultural setting. It recognizes that people's ideas of health, wellbeing, and healing are shaped by their cultural origins, which influence their choices for therapeutic methods and techniques.

Important Considerations for Adapting Somatic Practices:

1. Cultural Relevance: Somatic techniques must be consistent with the cultural beliefs, traditions, and therapeutic methods of the populations they serve. Practitioners should think about how somatic treatments might be combined with culturally appropriate rituals, ceremonies, and indigenous healing traditions to increase their efficacy and cultural resonance.

2. Language & Communication: Clear communication is key for making somatic activities accessible and culturally acceptable. Practitioners should use language that is understandable, inclusive, and supportive of their clients' linguistic choices and communication methods. Furthermore, practitioners should be aware of nonverbal signs and gestures that may have cultural importance, and adjust their communication appropriately.

3. Flexibility and Adaptability: Somatic practitioners must be versatile in their approach, understanding that varied cultural situations may need changes to standard somatic procedures. This might be introducing other movement styles, music, art, or narrative into somatic therapies to better match clients' cultural backgrounds and preferences.

4. Collaboration and Co-Creation: Working with clients and community members is vital for developing culturally sensitive somatic therapies.

Practitioners should actively seek advice and feedback from clients on how somatic treatments might be tailored to better match their cultural requirements and preferences. This collaborative approach promotes empowerment, ownership, and trust in the therapeutic interaction.

Practical Strategies for Adopting Somatic Practices:

1. Cultural Consultation: Speaking with cultural specialists, community leaders, and healers may give useful insights on the cultural relevance and acceptability of somatic practices in certain cultural settings.

2. Cultural Immersion: Immersing oneself in the cultural traditions, rituals, and practices of the populations served will help practitioners get a better knowledge and respect for cultural variety, which will shape their approach to adopting somatic techniques.

3. Pilot trying: By trying somatic therapies in multiple cultural settings, practitioners may obtain feedback, measure efficacy, and make necessary changes to guarantee cultural relevance and resonance.

4. Continuing Education: Ongoing education and training on cultural competency and diversity concerns provides practitioners with the information and skills required to successfully adapt somatic therapies to varied cultural settings.

Ethical Considerations for Cross-Cultural Somatic Work

Cross-cultural somatic work poses distinct ethical problems and concerns that practitioners must address in order to provide culturally sensitive and responsible treatment. This chapter delves into the ethical principles and rules that govern cross-cultural somatic work, highlighting the value of cultural competency, respect for diversity, and client autonomy.

Respect For Cultural Diversity:

Respect for cultural variety is an important ethical element in cross-cultural somatic practice. Practitioners must identify and respect the cultural ideas, values, and practices of clients from all origins, and avoid imposing their own cultural standards or assumptions on their experiences. This includes carefully listening to clients' viewpoints, recognizing their cultural identities, and participating in continuous self-reflection to detect and remove prejudices.

Cultural competence:

Cultural competency is required for delivering effective and ethical somatic treatment in cross-cultural settings. Practitioners must have the knowledge, skills, and awareness necessary to traverse cultural differences, communicate successfully across cultural borders, and tailor somatic therapies to clients' cultural backgrounds and preferences. This may need continual education, training, and consulting to improve cultural competency and close knowledge or understanding gaps.

Informed consent:

Informed consent is a critical component of ethical practice in somatic therapy, requiring practitioners to get specific permission from clients before beginning treatment. In cross-cultural settings, informed consent must include language limitations, literacy levels, and cultural variations in therapy procedures and limits. Practitioners should give clear and accessible information regarding the aim, risks, benefits, and alternatives to somatic therapies, allowing clients to make educated choices about their care.

Confidence and Privacy:

secrecy and privacy are critical in cross-cultural somatic treatment, and practitioners must protect clients' personal information while maintaining absolute secrecy in compliance with professional norms and regulatory requirements. Practitioners must be conscious of cultural variances in privacy and confidentiality standards, as well as clients' choices for information sharing and storage.

Cultural Humility and Self-reflection:

Cultural humility is acknowledging one's own limits, prejudices, and advantages but also committing to continuous self-reflection, learning, and progress. Practitioners must approach cross-cultural somatic treatment with humility, recognizing that they are not experts on their clients' cultural experiences and viewpoints. Instead, they should approach customers with openness, curiosity, and respect, aiming to understand and learn from their cultural origins and life experiences.

Ethical issues in cross-cultural somatic work necessitate practitioners to adhere to the ideals of respect, cultural competency, informed consent, confidentiality, and cultural humility. By emphasising cultural awareness, client autonomy, and ethical practice, practitioners may guarantee that cross-cultural somatic work fosters respect, dignity, and well-being for clients from various cultural backgrounds. Practitioners that engage in continual education, contemplation, and cooperation may traverse the intricacies of cross-cultural somatic work with integrity, compassion, and ethical integrity.

Chapter 9: Self-Care Practices for Somatic Awareness.

In the field of somatic therapy, practitioners often emphasise their clients' well-being, but it is also critical for practitioners to prioritise their own self-care. Self-care techniques for somatic awareness help practitioners grow mindfulness, manage stress, and preserve their physical and emotional health. This chapter delves into numerous self-care methods that increase somatic awareness and help practitioners in their therapeutic work.

1. Mindful Breathing: One of the most basic and effective self-care techniques is mindful breathing. Practitioners may spend a few minutes during the day focusing on their breath, observing the sensations of inhaling and expelling. This technique helps to relax the nervous system, decrease tension, and promote present-moment awareness, which improves somatic awareness and grounds practitioners in their bodies.

2. Body Scan Meditation: Body scan meditation is carefully drawing attention to various sections of the body and noting any feelings, tension, or pain. Practitioners may use body scan meditation into their daily practice to reconnect with their bodies, relieve stress, and develop a stronger connection to their somatic experience. This technique increases self-awareness and may assist practitioners in identifying areas of physical or mental stress that need attention.

3. Movement and Exercise: Regular movement and exercise are critical for both physical and mental well-being. Practitioners may engage in activities they love, such as yoga, walking, dancing, or strength training. Movement activities not only improve physical health but also increase somatic awareness by connecting practitioners to their bodies' feelings and rhythms.

4. Somatic Experiencing: Somatic experiencing is the purposeful focus on physical sensations and emotions, enabling them to be felt and processed without judgement or resistance. Practitioners may use somatic experience methods during times of stress or overload by tuning into their bodies and allowing feelings to occur and dissolve spontaneously. This technique promotes resilience, self-regulation, and emotional equilibrium.

5. Creative Expression: Creative pursuits like painting, music, dancing, and writing may be beneficial to practitioners' well-being. Creative expression enables practitioners to express their emotions, explore their inner worlds, and access their intrinsic creativity. By expressing oneself artistically, practitioners may relieve stress, acquire insight into their experiences, and build a feeling of pleasure and contentment.

6. Boundary Setting: In somatic therapy, setting clear limits is critical for preserving balance and avoiding burnout. Practitioners must emphasise their own needs and constraints, and communicate openly with clients and colleagues about their availability, workload, and self-care routines. Establishing appropriate limits allows practitioners to safeguard their energy, maintain their well-being, and keep their ability to help others.

Developing Resilience and Self-Compassion.

In the challenging area of somatic therapy, practitioners must cultivate resilience and self-compassion in order to overcome adversities, maintain their well-being, and flourish in their professional positions. This chapter investigates ways for developing resilience and self-compassion to help practitioners in their therapeutic practice.

1. Mindfulness is an essential practice for developing resilience and self-compassion. By bringing awareness to the present moment without judgement, practitioners may build resilience by embracing painful emotions and experiences as they happen. Mindfulness promotes self-compassion by urging practitioners to be kind and understanding of themselves, even when they are struggling.

2. **Embracing Imperfection:** Recognizing and embracing one's own flaws is critical to developing resilience and self-compassion. Practitioners must recognize that they are human and subject to errors, setbacks, and limits. By accepting imperfection, practitioners may develop resilience by learning from mistakes and setbacks, as well as self-compassion by being kind and forgiving to oneself.

3. **Establishing Support Networks**: Developing strong support networks is essential for resilience and self-compassion. Practitioners should look for

colleagues, mentors, friends, and family members who can provide support, understanding, and perspective at difficult times. Practitioners may increase their resilience and cultivate self-compassion by seeking help from others via connection and affirmation.

4. Practising Self-Care: Prioritising self-care is critical for developing resilience and self-compassion. Practitioners should schedule time for activities that promote their bodily, emotional, and spiritual well-being, such as exercise, hobbies, relaxation, or time spent in nature. Investing in self-care allows practitioners to replenish their energy reserves, alleviate stress, and build a feeling of balance and purpose.

5. Cultivating appreciation: Expressing appreciation is an effective strategy for increasing resilience and self-compassion. Practitioners may foster gratitude by consistently reflecting on what they are thankful for in their personal and professional life. By concentrating on the good parts of their experiences, practitioners may alter their viewpoint from scarcity to plenty, increasing resilience and cultivating self-compassion.

6. Seeking Professional growth: Constantly seeking professional growth and learning opportunities is critical for resilience and self-care. Practitioners should engage in continuing education, supervision, and consultation to improve their abilities, knowledge, and confidence in their therapeutic practice. Embracing development and learning allows practitioners to adapt to difficulties, overcome hurdles, and develop resilience in the face of adversity.

Rituals of Grounding and Centering

Grounding and centering rituals are essential in somatic therapy practice because they help practitioners connect with themselves, foster presence, and establish a feeling of stability in the face of therapeutic demands. Grounding and centering rituals provide practitioners techniques for anchoring themselves in the present moment, regulating their nervous systems, and maintaining a grounded presence with clients. This chapter looks at several rituals that practitioners might adopt into their everyday routines to enhance grounding and centering.

1. Morning Meditation: Beginning each day with a morning meditation routine helps practitioners feel grounded and focused. This practice is spending a few seconds after awakening to sit quietly, breathe deeply, and bring awareness to the body and breath. Visualisation methods, such as envisioning roots spreading from their feet into the soil, may help practitioners develop a feeling of solidity and connection to the ground.

2. Grounding techniques: Grounding techniques entail using the senses to connect with both the physical body and the surroundings. Practitioners may practise walking barefoot on grass or sand, feeling the texture under their feet, or resting their hands on solid surfaces like trees or rocks to receive grounding energy. Grounding methods make practitioners feel anchored and supported, which promotes a feeling of safety and stability.

3. Centering Breaths: Centering breaths are simple but effective strategies for increasing awareness of the breath and soothing the nervous system. Deep belly breathing, which involves inhaling deeply through the nose and expelling slowly through the mouth, may help practitioners centre themselves and release stress. Centering breaths create calm, clarity, and presence, which aids practitioners in staying focused and clear throughout therapeutic sessions.

4. Ritualized Movement: Practices like yoga, tai chi, and qigong may help you feel more grounded and centred. These practices blend breathwork with moderate, focused movements to promote awareness, balance, and harmony in the body. Practitioners may include movement rituals into their daily routines to relieve stress, develop flexibility, and improve body awareness.

5. appreciation Rituals: Cultivating appreciation via daily rituals may help practitioners anchor and centre themselves by moving their attention away from anxieties and pressures and into the present moment. Practitioners might engage in gratitude rituals by maintaining a gratitude diary, meditating on three things they are thankful for every day, or expressing appreciation via prayer or meditation. Gratitude rituals provide a feeling of abundance, connection, and well-being, helping practitioners maintain a happy and resilient mentality.

6. Closing Rituals: Concluding the day with a ritual assists practitioners in transitioning from work to rest and relaxation. This ritual might include lighting a candle, taking a few deep breaths, and expressing thanks for the day's events. Practitioners may create goals for peaceful sleep and self-care to ensure they leave the day feeling grounded, focused, and fed.

Strategies to Maintain Boundaries and Prevent Burnout

In the area of somatic therapy, practitioners must maintain limits and avoid burnout in order to preserve their well-being and efficacy in therapeutic work. Boundaries defend against emotional weariness and overload, while burnout prevention tactics emphasise self-care and resilience. This chapter discusses numerous ways that practitioners may use to establish appropriate limits and avoid burnout.

1. set Clear Boundaries: The first step in preserving boundaries is to set clear standards and expectations for client interactions. Practitioners should express their availability, session length, and scope of practice up front, establishing limits for scheduling, communication outside of sessions, and professional duties. Clear limits provide a feeling of safety and predictability to both practitioners and clients, lowering the likelihood of boundary breaches and fatigue.

2. Practice Self-Awareness: Practitioners must develop self-awareness in order to notice when their boundaries are being questioned or breached. This entails identifying physical, mental, and energy indicators that suggest tension, weariness, or discomfort. By responding to these signals and accepting their own limits, practitioners may take proactive actions to prioritise self-care and change their boundaries as required to preserve balance and well-being.

3. Use Supervision and Consultation: Regular supervision and consultation give excellent chances for practitioners to reflect on their work, seek direction, and work through difficult instances. Supervisors and colleagues may provide guidance, affirmation, and support as practitioners manage complicated ethical quandaries, boundary concerns, and burnout. Supervision also functions as a check and balance mechanism, ensuring that practitioners follow ethical rules and maintain healthy limits.

4. Establish Personal and Professional limits: Practitioners must establish limits in both their professional interactions and their personal life. This entails scheduling time for self-care, hobbies, and relationships outside of work in order to refuel and restore energy reserves. Practitioners should emphasise activities that promote their bodily, mental, and spiritual well-being, ensuring they have the resilience and resources to continue their therapeutic work in the long run.

5. Practise Regular Self-Care: Self-care is essential for avoiding burnout and sustaining resilience in somatic therapy practice. Practitioners should emphasise activities that promote relaxation, stress reduction, and emotional control, such as meditation, exercise, hobbies, and outdoor activities. Regular self-care routines restore practitioners' energy reserves, decrease stress, and improve general well-being, allowing them to be completely present and involved in their therapeutic work.

6. Practice Self-Compassion: Practitioners must develop self-compassion to combat emotions of inadequacy, perfectionism, and self-criticism, all of which lead to burnout. Self-compassion entails treating oneself with love, acceptance, and understanding, especially during times of stress or struggle. Practitioners may develop self-compassion via mindfulness practices, self-reflection, and reframing negative self-talk, which promotes resilience and emotional well-being in the face of stress.

Conclusion: Embracing Embodied Healing: Empowering You to Embody Wellness and Thrive

As you reach the end of this comprehensive guide to somatic therapy, you've embarked on a journey of self-discovery and empowerment. Through the exploration of somatic techniques, mind-body connections, and strategies for self-care and resilience, you've gained valuable insights into the holistic approach to healing that somatic therapy offers.

Throughout this journey, you've discovered the profound wisdom of the mind-body-spirit connection and the innate healing potential within your own body. By tuning into bodily sensations, emotions, and patterns, you've learned to harness your body's natural ability to heal and regulate itself.

You've also recognized the importance of maintaining healthy boundaries, prioritising self-care, and preventing burnout in your somatic therapy practice. By becoming more self-aware, setting clear boundaries, and engaging in regular self-care rituals, you can sustain your well-being and effectiveness in your therapeutic work, fostering greater resilience and longevity in your career.

As you reflect on the insights and practices shared in this guide, you're empowered to embody wellness and thrive in your life. Whether you're seeking relief from anxiety, stress, or trauma, or simply looking to deepen your connection to yourself and others, you have a wealth of tools and resources at your disposal to support your journey towards greater health and vitality.

In embracing embodied healing, you're invited to cultivate a deeper connection to your body, harness the power of your breath, movement, and awareness, and embrace a holistic approach to well-being that encompasses mind, body, and spirit. By integrating somatic techniques and principles into your daily life, you can unlock your innate potential for healing and transformation, leading to a life of greater balance, resilience, and joy.